IMAGES
of America

LAKE GEORGE

Gazebos in a wide variety of quaint Victorian and rustic Adirondack architectural styles dotted the lake's shoreline. This elaborate gazebo was located at Nirvana, the estate built by John Boulton Simpson on Green Island. (Courtesy of Hugh Allen Wilson.)

On the cover: The Lake View House. (Courtesy of the Bolton Historical Museum.)

IMAGES
of America

LAKE GEORGE

Gale J. Halm and Mary H. Sharp

ARCADIA

First published 2000
Reprinted 2000, 2001, 2002, 2004

Published by Arcadia Publishing,
Charleston SC, Chicago IL, Portsmouth NH, San Francisco CA

Printed in Great Britain

Library of Congress Catalog Card Number: 00-104040

For all general information, contact Arcadia Publishing:
Telephone 843-853-2070
Fax 843-853-0044
E-mail sales@arcadiapublishing.com
For customer service and orders:
Toll-free 1-888-313-2665

Visit us on the Internet at www.arcadiapublishing.com

We gratefully acknowledge permission to reproduce images from the following:

Bolton Historical Museum, Bolton Landing, New York
The Collection of Brookside, Saratoga County Historical Society (SCHS), Ballston Spa, New York
The Chapman Historical Museum, Glens Falls, New York
Crandall Public Library's Center for Folklife, History, and Cultural Programs, Glens Falls, New York
Collection of the Fort Ticonderoga Museum, Ticonderoga, New York
Hillview Free Library, Diamond Point, New York
Lake George Steamboat Company, Lake George, New York
Silver Bay Association, Silver Bay, New York
Clifton F. West Historical Museum, Hague, New York
Wiawaka Holiday House Inc., Lake George, New York
Hugh Allen Wilson, Bolton Landing, New York

(Credit for individual photographs is given within parenthesis following the text.)

CONTENTS

The magnificent white birch is another of nature's gifts that has been generously bestowed at Lake George.

INTRODUCTION

The form and natural beauty of Lake George are the result of geological development and glacial sculpting that shaped a much larger region over the time span of a billion or more years. The lake's location between the headwaters of the Hudson River and the north-flowing Lake Champlain gave it strategic importance along the early water highway connecting New York and Montreal before roads existed through the wilderness. Fierce struggles were fought between Native American nations and French, British, and Colonial troops for control of the lake and ultimately of North America.

The names by which the lake has been known reflect the diverse national interests. To the Iroquois who laid claim to the territory, it was An-Di-A-Ta-Roc-Te (the-lake-that-shuts-itself-in). On May 30, 1646, it was renamed Lac du Saint Sacrement (the Lake of the Blessed Sacrament) by the French Jesuit missionary and martyr Fr. Issac Jogues in commemoration of the Feast of Corpus Christi. The lake carried the French name for 109 years until British Gen. Sir William Johnson renamed it Lake George on August 28, 1755, in honor of His Majesty George II of England. With anti-British sentiment still prevailing in the early 1800s, James Fenimore Cooper's campaign to promote the more "appropriate" name Horicon (Silvery Water) received significant support, but the name, which he had used in his book *The Last of the Mohicans*, was not adopted.

The region was unsafe for settlement until after the Revolutionary War, and it was not until after the Civil War that Lake George became a resort community. There were only six hotels and one steamboat, the *Minne-Ha-Ha*, on the lake in 1865 when Seneca Ray Stoddard arrived in Glens Falls, New York, and turned his attention to the fields of landscape painting and outdoor photography—work in which he specialized for the rest of his career. Advertisements for his early stereoscopic views of the lake appeared in Glens Falls newspapers by 1867.

For 50 years, Stoddard artistically documented the Adirondack landscape, architecture, and leisure lifestyle at lakeside resorts with cameras that he built himself. His visual record of the times and its people is particularly remarkable since most photography was still limited to studio work, due to the difficult and time-consuming tasks involved; however, Stoddard, the pioneer landscape photographer, was carrying his bulky and cumbersome equipment to remote locations and developing his heavy glass-plate negatives wherever his subject matter required. His work received early national and international recognition.

Much of what we know about the social history of the period is preserved in his photographs. In addition to this wonderful visual record, Stoddard also published yearly guidebooks of the

Adirondacks and Lake George that provide an excellent verbal supplement to the people, places, and events that he photographed. The first edition of the Lake George guide appeared in 1873; updated versions continued for four decades. The guidebooks, with humorous passages written in the style of Mark Twain, are quoted frequently in our text.

Jesse Sumner Wooley, a second pioneer photographer to whom we are indebted, operated a prominent studio in Ballston Spa throughout his career, as well as an additional shop at Silver Bay on Lake George during the summer seasons of 1908 through 1923. His photographs preserve a great deal of the history of both areas. In the summers of 1893, 1894, and 1895, Wooley worked as Stoddard's assistant on photographic tours of the Adirondacks, Vermont, and the Hudson River. Together and individually, they promoted and capitalized on the tourist industry. In the process, they also created an invaluable resource for posterity. Peruse with us a sampling of the rich Lake George pictorial legacy that was recorded in the decades preceding and immediately following the turn of the past century by the lenses of these and other remarkably capable photographers. Without these pioneers, this book would not have been possible.

Left: Seneca Ray Stoddard lived from 1843 to 1917. (Courtesy of The Chapman Historical Museum.) *Right*: Jesse Sumner Wooley was born in 1867 and died in 1943. (Courtesy of Brookside, SCHS.)

We gratefully acknowledge the assistance provided by the following institutions and staff members: Director Patricia S. Babé, Bolton Historical Museum; Director Todd DeGarmo and Albert Fowler, Crandall Public Library's Center for Folklife, History, and Cultural Programs; William P. Dow, Lake George Steamboat Company; The "Anthony D. Pell" Curator of Collections Christopher D. Fox, Fort Ticonderoga Museum; Curators of Collections Rebecca Gereau and Alexandra D. McKee, The Chapman Historical Museum; Director Martha Havens, Hillview Free Library; Executive Director Mark C. Johnson, Silver Bay Association; Executive Director Suzie Kilpatrick and Curator of Collections Christine Heidorf, Brookside, Saratoga County Historical Society; Director Clifton F. West, Clifton F. West Historical Museum; and Mary Bitel and Associates of Wiawaka Holiday House. For their contribution of material, we also gratefully acknowledge the following: Hugh Allen Wilson, Michael Tobey and Ann Shakeshaft, Jody Edson, Fred Chase, Mark Spitzer, and Dave and Marge Comstock. To the following, we extend our thanks for providing helpful information: Gail Malcolm of the Lake George Club, Linda Goodwin of the Adirondack Camp, Ted Shuster, David Martucci, Lois Tucker, and Ethel Andrus. To our patient friends who have not forgotten us while we have been involved in this project, we also give our thanks. And, above all, to Dick and Jules, who endured interrupted schedules and houses of chaos, we are appreciative of your useful suggestions, moral support, extraordinary proofreading, and the fact that you were always there when needed. In conclusion, we dedicate this book to our grandchildren with the hope that from its pages they will come to know and appreciate this special place that has meant so much to us.

—Gale J. Halm and Mary H. Sharp

One
THE WATER HIGHWAY

Welcome to Lake George, the "Queen of American Lakes." Although this familiar description may suggest recent publicity to some, the phrase dates back to the 1800s. In 1866, Thomas Nelson referred to the "Queen of Waters" in his guide to Lake George and Lake Champlain. Later, Seneca Ray Stoddard used the phrase "Queen of American Lakes," as did the *Lake George Mirror*, which carried the title in its banner by the beginning of the 20th century. Nelson also wrote that the islands appeared to be "resting, if the weather be calm, on their own reflected images." (Wooley.)

During the geological formation of the Adirondack Region, two ancient rivers flowed through the area that later became the Lake George basin. They were separated by a mountain barrier that formed two watersheds in the present vicinity of the Narrows. One river flowed south from the Northwest Bay and made its way to the Hudson River by way of the lowlands that existed between the present Pilot Knob and French Mountain. The second river flowed north from the mountain divide and made its way through a valley west of Rogers Rock to Lake Champlain. The rivers flowed in this manner until glaciers buried most of New York State in many thousand feet of ice. The advancing and receding glaciers ground the tops of mountains and carried the loosened soil and rocks with them in the ice. When the ice mass melted, large deposits of the released debris blocked the exits of the north- and south-flowing rivers. The water that was trapped slowly filled the basin and covered the mountain barrier in the Narrows. Eventually, the new lake created an outlet at the LaChute River in Ticonderoga and flowed northward into Lake Champlain.

The Narrow Tongue and Black from Shelving Lake George

In the photograph above, the path of the former south-flowing river can be seen in the upper center on page 10. Here, the Northwest Bay flows into the lake behind the point of Tongue Mountain. The numerous islands are remnants of the pre-glacial mountain barrier that existed in the Narrows. The former north-flowing river continues its path into the distance on the right of page 11. As a result of the glacial sculpting that created Lake George, a long continuous water chain was formed, linking the Hudson River, Lake George, Lake Champlain, and the St. Lawrence River. Only three portages were required between the present port of New York City and the French settlements on the St. Lawrence River. The total carrying distance was approximately 15 and 20 miles. The water highway became an important transportation and trading route with international implications. Furs that left the New World from the Hudson were shipped to England. Furs that left the St. Lawrence went to France. Control of the water highway meant control of trade and expansion of empire for either France or Britain. Lake George held a very strategic position. (Wooley; courtesy of the Silver Bay Association.)

The French pushed down from Canada on Lake Champlain and built Fort St. Frederick at Crown Point in 1731. British garrisons continued to move farther up the Hudson Valley. Lake George was an unsafe no-man's-land in between the two opposing forces and became the scene of violent struggles, as Great Britain and France vied for control of the wilderness. (Courtesy of Hugh Allen Wilson.)

British Gen. William Johnson planned to establish a post at Ticonderoga and attack the French at Crown Point. Before he could proceed, the French under Baron Dieskau formed an ambush just south of Lake George on September 8, 1755. Col. Ephram Williams was among those killed in the daylong battle. His estate provided for the establishment of Williams College. In 1854, alumni erected this monument near the battle site.

On the monument: BATTLE OF LAKE GEORGE SEPT 1755

Plaque: DEFEAT WOULD HAVE OPENED THE ROAD TO ALBANY TO THE FRENCH

While allied with the British, Mohawk Chief King Hendrick was among those killed in the Battle of Lake George on September 8, 1755. He and Sir William Johnson are honored on the monument pictured. Despite early losses, Johnson's provincial army prevailed over the French and their Iroquois allies. The British spent the remainder of the season building Fort William Henry.

In August 1757, the fort was besieged by French troops under Marquis de Montcalm and members of an Iroquois confederacy. The fort surrendered six days later. Conditions of the surrender permitted safe conduct to Fort Edward. However, Montcalm was unable to control the Iroquois and a massacre occurred. Following the incident, England resolved to resume the offensive.

The Lake George Battle Monument was erected by the Society of Colonial Wars of the State of New York and was unveiled on September 8, 1903, with imposing civic and military ceremonies. The figures representing Gen. William Johnson and Mohawk Chief King Hendrick are made of bronze and stand on a granite pedestal. The inscription on the west side of the base reads in bold letters, "Battle of Lake George. Sept. 8, 1755." On the north side overlooking the lake is the following inscription: "Confidence inspired by this victory was of inestimable value to the American army in the war of the Revolution." The inscription on the east reads, "1903. The Society of Colonial Wars erected this monument to commemorate the victory of the Colonial forces under General William Johnson and their Mohawk allies under Chief Hendrick over the French regulars commanded by Baron Dieskau with their Canadian and Indian allies." The south face says, "Defeat would have opened the road to Albany to the French." (Courtesy of the Crandall Public Library.)

Throngs gathered at Fort Ticonderoga on Monday, May 10, 1875, for the centennial celebration of the capture of Fort Ticonderoga by Ethan Allen and the Green Mountain Boys. The program for the day included a 100-gun salute at sunrise, a procession over the route taken by Ethan Allen, and speeches urging the preservation and restoration of the historic site, which had deteriorated in the preceding century. Following the Revolutionary War, all land held by the British Crown became the property of the state in which it was located. Ownership of Fort Ticonderoga was transferred to New York State in 1790, and the state, in turn, deeded the property to Columbia and Union Colleges for educational purposes in 1803. William Ferris Pell became interested in the property and was able to purchase the land from the colleges in 1820. He built a home, known as The Pavilion, tended the grounds, curtailed the removal of wagon loads of stone and other materials, and did what he could to prevent the further deterioration of the fort. (Courtesy of the Collection of the Fort Ticonderoga Museum.)

Through the efforts of the Ticonderoga Historical Society, national support was gathered for a bill introduced to Congress in 1898 that sought to have the federal government acquire and restore Fort Ticonderoga. That bill and a subsequent bill in 1906 failed to pass. On September 2, 1908, the Ticonderoga Historical Society and the New York State Historical Association continued their efforts on behalf of the fort. They hosted a clambake for the press of the Champlain, Mohawk, and Hudson Valleys in hopes of generating support for submitting to Congress a third bill for the preservation of the site.

CLAM BAKE AT FORT TICONDEROGA, N.Y. SEPT. 2nd 1908.

The press gathered at the fort for the clambake and the speeches. An address by the Honorable Robert O. Bascom, secretary of the New York State Historical Association, called upon all citizens to preserve the heritage of this historic place for all future generations. Alfred C. Bossom displayed architectural drawings for the reconstruction of the old fort, based on his research. Additional guests were limited to 150. They paid $2 per ticket to help offset the expense of the clambake for the press.

Stephen H.P. Pell, who had fond childhood memories of visiting his grandmother at The Pavilion and playing among the ruins of the fort, was present at the 1908 clambake with his wife, Sarah G.T. Pell. They were inspired by the speeches and intrigued by the architectural sketches that were proposed. Since repeated efforts had failed to interest the state and national governments to care for the fort, and the owner's willingness to sell at a nominal price if preservation was guaranteed had not been accepted, Mr. and Mrs. Pell decided to undertake the restoration of the fort and the rehabilitation of The Pavilion themselves. In-depth research located documents providing accurate details for historically correct reconstruction, and within the year, work was under way. On July 6, 1909, the Fort Ticonderoga Museum was dedicated with Pres. William Howard Taft, French Ambassador Jesserand, and British Ambassador Bryce in attendance. Taft is pictured above on the lower step of The Pavilion. He is flanked by museum founders Sarah and Stephen Pell. (Courtesy of the Collection of the Fort Ticonderoga Museum.)

By the time of the July 6, 1909 dedication, the restoration of the fort had progressed to the point shown above. Forty-five workers were involved in the project, and some order had been made of the ruins. At the time, the estimated cost of reconstruction according to the architect's plans was $500,000 and the estimated time required to complete the restoration was ten years. Millions of dollars and 90 years later, restoration and reconstruction continues.

An inspection of the fort was included in the dedication activities. President Taft is pictured above in the center. To the left of Taft is Col. Robert M. Thompson, father of Mrs. Pell and the founder of the International Nickel Company, whose generous contributions provided the funding to rebuild the fort. To the right of Taft is Alfred C. Bossom (holding papers), whose initial research and interest led to his selection as the architect of the restoration of the fort.

t. Defiance   Outlet of Lake George   The Flag Bastion   Fort Ticondero Bay

In 1755, Marquis de Vaudreuil, the governor of New France, commissioned Marquis de Lotbiniere to construct a fort that would guard passage along the water highway between Lake George and Lake Champlain. The fort was built with the hope that it would prevent the British from gaining a foothold farther north. Fort Carillon withstood its first British assault. British Gen. James Abercromby, Lord Howe as second in command, and a force of 15,000 men embarked from the site of Fort William Henry on July 5, 1758, in over 900 bateaux, whaleboats, and other craft. The success of their campaign to capture Fort Carillon depended on the tactical ability of Lord Howe. The loss of Howe in an early skirmish and the ineptitude of Abercromby resulted in the complete failure of the expedition. After repeated ineffectual attacks, the huge British force fell back from the vastly outnumbered French under the Marquis de Montcalm. The British retreated in disarray to their camp at the south end of Lake George.

Underground   Court Yard or "Place

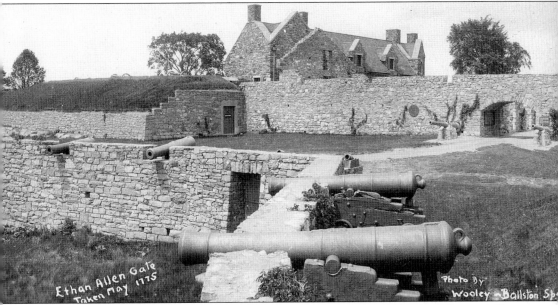

In July 1759, with British Gen. Jeffrey Amherst in command, 11,000 men besieged Fort Carillon and succeeded where Abercromby had failed. The French retreated after setting fire to the fort and blowing up the powder magazine. Amherst rebuilt the fort and renamed it Fort Ticonderoga. The fort saw no further action until the morning of May 10, 1775, when Ethan Allen and his Green Mountain Boys surprised the small British force and demanded the surrender of the fort "in the name of the Great Jehovah and the Continental Congress." Continental troops held the fort until July 5, 1777, when British troops under Gen. John Burgoyne fortified Mount Defiance with cannons aimed at the fort, and the Colonials withdrew. When Burgoyne surrendered at Saratoga in October, the small garrison remaining at Fort Ticonderoga burned the fort and escaped to Canada. The remains were allowed to deteriorate until the Pell restoration, which is pictured here *c.* 1925. (Wooley.)

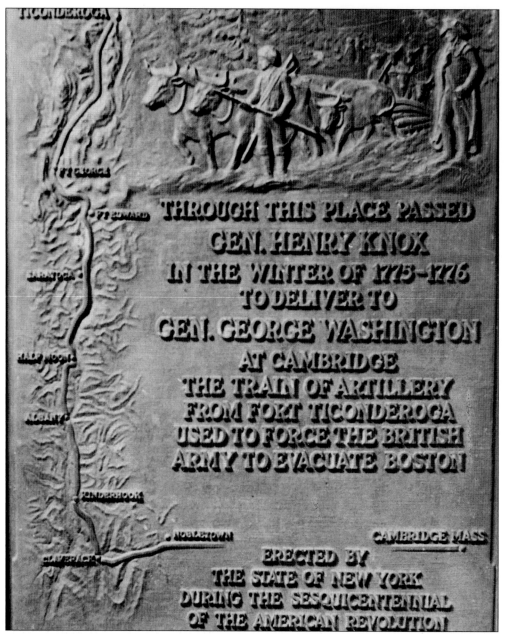

THROUGH THIS PLACE PASSED
GEN. HENRY KNOX
IN THE WINTER OF 1775-1776
TO DELIVER TO
GEN. GEORGE WASHINGTON
AT CAMBRIDGE
THE TRAIN OF ARTILLERY
FROM FORT TICONDEROGA
USED TO FORCE THE BRITISH
ARMY TO EVACUATE BOSTON

ERECTED BY
THE STATE OF NEW YORK
DURING THE SESQUICENTENNIAL
OF THE AMERICAN REVOLUTION

In the early days of the Revolutionary War, Gen. Henry Knox was sent to Fort Ticonderoga by Gen. George Washington to obtain the British cannons that had been captured by Ethan Allen and the Green Mountain Boys. His mission was to transport them to the Colonial troops in Boston for use in their efforts to drive the British from the town. The artillery train left Ticonderoga in early December 1775 with more than 50 tons of weapons. In the harsh winter weather, the cannons were rowed on makeshift vessels and dragged by oxen and horses on sleds for hundreds of miles over wilderness routes and mountainous terrain. By the sheer determination of Knox and his men, the weapons reached Boston in late January 1776. They were instrumental in forcing the British to evacuate Boston on March 17, 1776. This plaque marking the route taken by Knox is located at Sabbath Day Point.

Two

TRANSPORTATION

Soon after Robert Fulton's steamboat *Clermont* made its historic 150-mile, 32-hour trip up the Hudson River from New York City to Albany in 1807, other steamboats and travelers began to follow in increasing numbers. Gradually, the ports of New York City, Albany, and Troy became terminals, with several steamboat companies operating a schedule of Hudson River day boats and night lines. Before trains met the steamboats at the northern ports, stagecoach lines provided the best option for service to Lake George; the distance was approximately 70 miles—at least a full day's journey. Travel was difficult and passengers bounced along over old, rough military roads and rutted trails. In dry weather, the roads were dusty; in wet weather, carriages became mired in the mud.

Rail service was gradually extended toward Lake George. A railroad spur from Fort Edward finally reached Glens Falls in 1869 and carried 12 trains a day. The Glens Falls station (pictured) was located at Maple and Walnut Streets. Lake George passengers continued their journey from that point by stagecoach via the plank road. The timbered roadway was made with planks 4 inches thick and 8 feet long that were laid crosswise to timbers, or sleepers, lying on a graded base beneath. (Courtesy of the Crandall Public Library.)

The plank road between Glens Falls and Lake George was privately built in the 1840s; two tollgates were located along the route. The second gate at French Mountain is pictured here c. 1879. Many of the plank road investors were also involved in the stagecoach companies that made extensive use of the road. A good day's traffic through the tollgate was about 50 vehicles. The plank road was considered one of the smoothest and best-tended roads in the country. (Stoddard; courtesy of The Chapman Historical Museum.)

GLENS FALLS & LAKE GEORGE
Stage Company.

NEW COACHES AND EQUIPMENTS, FAST HORSES.

LAKE GEORGE PASSENGERS

Who take this route will leave the Railroad at

GLENS FALLS,

And passing over the Plank road, will witness the exquisite river scenery of

GLENS FALLS,

So graphically described in Cooper's "Last of the Mohicans," the scenes of the Border Conflicts in the

OLD FRENCH WAR,

And will travel across the battle ground of

DIESKAU AND SIR WILLIAM JOHNSON.

The Stages connect with the three trains going North, and the Morning, Mid-day and Evening trains going South.

The Glens Falls and Lake George Stage Company operated its schedule in conjunction with the arrival and departure of all trains at Glens Falls and the steamers at Lake George. All of the through tickets were sold over this line. By special arrangement, the trains and the boats waited for the arrival of the stages, which carried passengers between the docks and the depot. The passengers' baggage was also checked through via the stagecoach line. Seneca Ray Stoddard wrote in his 1880 Lake George guide, "This line is probably excelled by none on the continent . . . Its elegant Concord and Tally-ho coaches, its handsome four and six-horse teams, with their experienced drivers, together with the rare beauty of the scenery and historic interests and associations along the way, afford opportunity for a most delightful coaching experience, which is not continued so long as ordinarily to become wearisome, but gives variety and is an ever to be remembered feature of the trip to Lake George."

The golden age of stagecoaches occurred in the Lake George area between 1869 and 1882. At that time, trains had reached as far as Glens Falls, but additional travel was still required to transport the increasing number of affluent visitors to the lake's hotels and steamboats. The elegant Concord coaches bounced along at a brisk top speed of 10 miles per hour, carrying from 15 to 20 passengers on top and from 8 to 12 inside, with space provided in the rear for baggage. The outside seats were preferable and, Seneca Ray Stoddard wrote with humor, were even rudely scrambled for unless rain threatened. It took one and one-quarter hours to make the 9-mile trip from Glens Falls to Lake George, with a stop often made at George Brown's well-known halfway house. The Fort William Henry Hotel served as the center for stagecoach activity at Lake George. A stagecoach office was located in the hotel livery, and a ticket office was located in the hotel lobby. (Courtesy of the Crandall Public Library.)

The whistle of the steam locomotive arriving at Caldwell, as the Town of Lake George was then known, on May 29, 1882, sounded the death knell for the stagecoach routes operating between Glens Falls and the lake. Discussion about railroad service over the well-traveled route had begun as early as 1832; however, it took 50 years before it was possible to make passage to Lake George—13 years after train service reached Glens Falls. Through a consolidation of interests, the Delaware and Hudson Company leased exclusive rights from rail and steam companies serving Lake George so that the lake was accessible only by the D & H Railroad lines. In 1909, ten trains arrived daily, and where railroad tracks ended, the D & H steamboat took over. The first Fort William Henry Hotel, which burned in 1909, is visible in the distance in the upper right-hand corner. (Courtesy of the Lake George Steamboat Company.)

The first steamboat launched on the lake was the *James Caldwell* in 1817. It had a brick smokestack and a top speed of 4 miles per hour, allowing it to travel the length of the lake in a day—almost as quickly as an oarsman could row the distance. The boat burned in 1821 and was replaced in 1824 by the *Mountaineer*, which had a top speed of 6 miles per hour. To save time en route, the captain stopped the side-wheeler only to take ladies on board. Men were expected to be rowed out and transferred to the yawl towed behind the steamer. The towline was pulled in and the passenger then climbed on deck without impeding headway. The *Mountaineer* operated with this approach until the boat was condemned in 1837. The *William Caldwell* was in service from 1838 to 1848. At 12 miles per hour, the boat was able to make a round-trip from Caldwell with a three-and-one-half-hour layover in Ticonderoga, allowing passengers to visit the fort ruins. In 1850, that ship was replaced by the *John Jay*, which burned on July 29, 1856, in Hague, with a loss of six lives. The *Minne-Ha-Ha*, pictured above, was built the following winter with engines and boilers salvaged from the *John Jay*. (Courtesy of the Crandall Public Library.)

LAKE GEORGE.

THE STEAMER
"MINNE-HA-HA,"

Captain E. S. HARRIS,

MAKES DAILY TRIPS THROUGH THE LAKE

connecting with the boats on

Lake Champlain, for Montreal, Quebec, Niagara, White and Franconia Mountains, Mount Mansfield,

and the Railway to

SARATOGA, TROY, ALBANY & NEW YORK.

THE

"MINNE-HA-HA"

Leaves her dock, at Caldwell, every morning, Sundays excepted, at 7½ o'clock—steams down the Lake among the Islands, and through to Ticonderoga, connecting with

LAKE CHAMPLAIN STEAMERS

GOING NORTH AND SOUTH,

Returning in the afternoon upon the arrival of the Lake Champlain Steamers, arriving at her dock at the Fort William Henry Hotel at 6 o'clock P. M.

The *Minne-Ha-Ha* began service in June 1857. The boat was able to travel at 13 miles per hour and carry 400 passengers. The name for the steamer was taken from Longfellow's poem "Hiawatha." Minne-Ha-Ha, translated as "laughing water," was the wife of the Native American chief about whom the poem was written. The 140-foot side-wheeler, the last wood-burning steamer on the lake, required six cords of wood for each ten-hour round-trip from Caldwell. The boat was taken out of service after the 1876 season. The ship's engine was removed, and the hull was sold and used as a floating 25-room hotel and dining facility for a few years at Black Mountain Point.

The 64-foot *Ganouskie* was built in 1869 and lengthened to 72 feet in 1870 to expand the steamboat service provided by the *Minne-Ha-Ha*. The *Ganouskie* left the north end of the lake each morning and arrived at Caldwell with passengers in time for the departure of the afternoon southbound stagecoach. Making stops along the way, it returned to its northern dock at about 6:00 p.m. The *Ganouskie*, pictured here at Crosbyside *c.* 1880, was retired after the 1883 season and was purchased for use as a floating saloon at Big Burnt Island. (Stoddard; courtesy of The Chapman Historical Museum.)

The 1,000-passenger *Horicon* was put into service in 1877 to replace the *Minne-Ha-Ha*. Its dock was in Caldwell, where the elegant 195-foot side-wheeler created such an increase in business that six-horse stagecoaches, instead of four-horse models, were needed to carry passengers between the dock and Glens Falls. The *Horicon*, pictured here at the Sagamore Hotel dock in 1895, was retired in 1911 after 34 years of service. (Courtesy of the Bolton Historical Museum.)

RUINS OF STR. TICONDEROGA, BURNED AUG. 29th 1901, LAKE GEORGE. N.Y.

The increase in tourism created by the 1882 arrival of train service to Caldwell taxed the capacity of the existing steamboats to the limit. In 1884, the 800-passenger *Ticonderoga* replaced the 60-passenger *Ganouskie*. In 1896, the wooden side-wheeler was lengthened to 187 feet to carry 1,000 passengers. On August 29, 1901, after departing Baldwin without passengers, a smoldering fire below the boiler deck of the *Ticonderoga* erupted into rapidly spreading flames. Within two hours, the boat had burned to water's edge.

Str. Sagamore and Her Record Breaking Crowd, Aug. 1906. Showing Tongue Mt. and Hundred Islands in the Distance, Lake George, N.Y.

The *Sagamore*, a name popularized by James Fenimore Cooper's *The Last of the Mohicans*, replaced the *Ticonderoga* in 1902. After the first season, the *Sagamore* was lengthened by 20 feet at midship to 223 feet to improve stability. The first steel-hulled steamer on the lake, it was the largest at that time, carrying 1,500 passengers. The boat was scrapped in 1937.

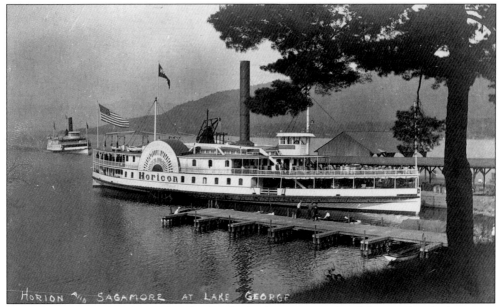

HORION AND SAGAMORE AT LAKE GEORGE

The *Horicon II*, the last side-wheeler built for use on the lake, replaced the aging *Horicon I* in 1911. Ceremonies up and down the lake welcomed its arrival. It was the largest, fastest, and most magnificent of the steamers launched on the lake and the pride of the fleet. The popular 231-foot steamer was able to carry 1,500 passengers. The year it was launched, the Horicon, together with the *Mohican II* and the *Sagamore*, carried a total of more than 120,000 passengers. (Wooley.)

GLENBURNIE NY. JULY 1ST 1927

On July 1, 1927, the *Sagamore* left the Baldwin dock on its morning run in a pea soup fog. It was proceeding by compass readings when the bow struck the ston e ledges of Anthony's Nose. Despite severe leaks in the hull, all passengers, mail, and freight were unloaded at the Glenburnie dock before the boat was purposely beached in 18 feet of water to prevent it from completely sinking. The *Sagamore* was raised and, after being reconditioned, was returned to service the following year.

In 1908, the wooden *Mohican I*, in service from 1894 to 1907, was replaced by the new steel-hulled *Mohican II*, pictured at the Lake George Village dock with the *Mountaineer*. The *Mohicans* were smaller than their sister ships and were primarily responsible for the popular Paradise Bay cruises. The *Mohican I* also took passengers to Fourteen Mile Island, which the Lake George Steamboat Company owned from 1888 to 1905 and used as a destination for daylong excursion parties. The *Mohican II* is still in service today. (Wooley; Brookside, SCHS.)

The second Delaware and Hudson station, pictured above, was built in 1911. It was an exciting time for rail travel; however, World War I, the development of the automobile, and the Great Depression were to have their effect. A decline in rail passengers led the D & H to discontinue service to Lake George on November 11, 1957. (Wooley.)

Early steamboats used a dock at Cook's Landing as their northern terminus. However, the number and size of the newer steamboats necessitated moving the northern landing site to Baldwin Landing. Pictured here at Baldwin, from left to right, are the steamers *Horicon*, *Mohican*, and *Sagamore*.

Baldwins Stage Coaches, "Watering" at Old Central House, Ticonderoga, N.Y. 1869.

Baldwin Landing was named in honor of the veteran stage driver William G. Baldwin, who owned a line of stagecoaches that provided transportation throughout the region. The stage route passed through the town of Ticonderoga, which was the area that early natives and trappers knew as the portage over which they carried their boats and supplies. The name Ticonderoga is said to be similar in sound to the Native American word that means or indicates "between two great waters."

In 1875, seven years before trains reached the Lake George tourist center of Caldwell, the Delaware and Hudson Railroad extended its tracks northward from Whitehall to Ticonderoga. The railroad also completed a 5-mile spur between Baldwin Landing on northern Lake George, pictured above, and the Montcalm Landing on Lake Champlain, pictured below. The Baldwin spur facilitated the transfer of passengers to and from Lake George and encouraged the growth of tourism in the region. Ticonderoga, rather than Whitehall, became the Lake Champlain steamer terminal.

The proximity of the Lake Champlain steamer dock, the junction of the Baldwin spur from Lake George, and the main railroad artery of the D & H between New York City and Montreal created a transportation network that allowed continuous rail and steamboat service between the two cities. This network permitted a coordination of scheduling and ease of transfer that was of benefit to the passenger as well as the company. (Wooley.)

Well-organized steamer crews scurried to move tons of baggage and freight at docks up and down the lake. In the pictures on this page, the staff of the Silver Bay Association lends a hand. The "elephant chain" of trunks is pictured above. The *Lake George Mirror* of July 4, 1902, reported that the steamer *Horicon*, while bringing 600 college women to a YWCA conference at Silver Bay, had never carried so much baggage on a single trip. (Wooley; courtesy of the Silver Bay Association.)

Steamers made New York morning newspapers available anywhere on the lake by noon and provided hotel supplies and express deliveries with regularity. A considerable amount of freight was shipped, including lumber and building materials for the Lake George construction boom, particularly to areas where no roads existed. Later, the *Sagamore*, *Horicon II*, and the *Mohican* began to carry automobiles when cars became numerous and the road over Tongue Mountain had not yet been improved. Together, the three steamers carried upwards of 1,000 vehicles a year during the 1920s. (Wooley.)

In 1870, the steamboat company received a contract to transport U.S. mail on the lake and began to deliver mailbags to the docks of the many hamlets and hotels that had their own post offices. Docks, where regularly scheduled stops were made, received four mail deliveries a day! James Adams, the postmaster, is pictured at the Silver Bay dock and on his way to the post office with the mailbags. Also shown are some of the early postmarks that were used by post offices around the lake.

Motorized transportation gradually replaced horses. Here, guests used the Malaney's Auto Bus Line to travel from the Ticonderoga railroad station to the Silver Bay Association Hotel. The open car with a surrey top provided little protection in cold and rainy weather. (Courtesy of the Silver Bay Association.)

The Glens Falls and Bolton Auto Stage Line is pictured above, *c.* 1910, in front of the Glens Falls Insurance Company building at Glen and Bay Streets. The express truck is one of the earliest examples of a motorized freight delivery system in the area. The horseless carriage supplemented the delivery of supplies received by steamboat. (Courtesy of the Crandall Public Library.)

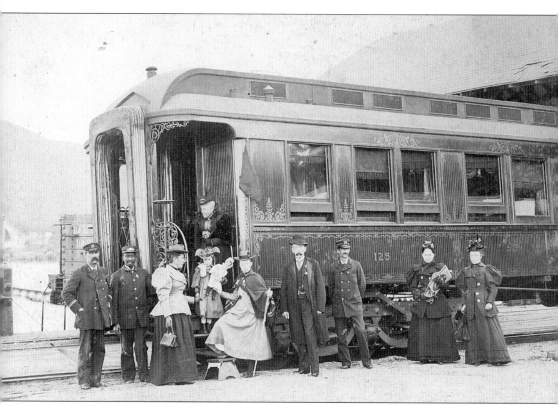

Great industrialists and members of society crisscrossed the country in their private railroad cars. Each car was self-contained, with living, dining, and sleeping facilities. The family of J.B. Simpson is pictured above, boarding their elaborately decorated private car on the Lake George steamer dock c. 1895. Simpson, fourth from the right, owned the yacht *Fanita*, which transported the family between the dock and Nirvana, their cottage estate on Green Island along the famous stretch known as Millionaires' Row. (Courtesy of Hugh Allen Wilson.)

Three
ACCOMMODATIONS

In the early 1800s, inns and taverns provided basic lodging for travelers who ventured into the Lake George region. As transportation improved and publications touted the lake's beauty, its historic relics, and its rejuvenating powers, tourists who had the means to linger expected more than modest shelters could provide. The Fort William Henry Hotel opened in June 1855 to provide affluent Lake George travelers elegant accommodations similar to those found in Saratoga. In 1868, the hotel was purchased by T. Roessle & Sons of Albany, who reconstructed and further enlarged the facility to produce the imposing structure pictured above. (Stoddard; courtesy of the Crandall Public Library.)

The 1868 Fort William Henry Hotel renovations included the addition of a 25-foot-wide piazza, which extended the entire 334-foot length of the hotel. The roof was supported by a colonnade of Corinthian columns 30 feet high. The impressive piazza was a favorite spot for guests to promenade, providing an opportunity to be seen, as well as to inspect the new guests with the arrival of each stagecoach. Seneca Ray Stoddard described making one's entrance as "walking the gauntlet." (Stoddard; courtesy of the Crandall Public Library.)

The Fort William Henry Hotel was unquestionably the social hub of the lake when these two pictures were taken in the early 1870s. Fashionably elegant and sometimes pretentious guests gathered on the piazza to mingle with other guests deemed suitable. They discussed social events and viewed the landscaped grounds, which were embellished with fountains and garden ornaments. The grounds overlooked the lake and the mountains beyond. (Stoddard; courtesy of the Crandall Public Library.)

LAKE GEORGE.

Fort William Henry Hotel

IS OPEN FOR THE RECEPTION OF GUESTS.

This Hotel has been completely rebuilt and refurnished, and now compares favorably with any first class Hotel in Europe or America. It is situated on the site of Fort William Henry, adjoining Fort George and the old French Battle Ground. The Building contains 450 rooms, which may be had in

Suites or Private Parlors, as Desired.

Water is carried to every part of the House, which is supplied with

COLD AND WARM BATHS.

The entire House is brilliantly lighted with gas made on the premises.

A Celebrated Band is Engaged for the Season.

THE TELEGRAPH

Connects with all lines through the State, and gives reports of the

STOCK MARKET THREE TIMES A DAY.

A Livery Stable is connected with the Hotel,

Together with an abundance of stable and barn room, for private horses and carriages. The drives on the Lake shore and through the surrounding country are unsurpassed.

FRENCH COACHES,

(With seats on top and rear) connect with the Glens Falls Railroad, also, with Adirondack Railroad at Warrensburgh. Time, one hour.

This graphic for the Fort William Henry Hotel is from an 1870 edition of B.C. Butler's *Lake George and Lake Champlain*. The Fort William Henry rates were generally higher than those found at most other hotels at the lake. The rates listed for the 1880s ranged among $17.50, $21, $25, and $28 per week, based on the size, location, and amenities of the room. Wages of the time were also comparably low, and vacations were a luxury; however, many of the guests at the lake stayed for extended periods.

The immense dining room had a grand view of the lake and the capacity to seat 1,000 guests comfortably. Sumptuous meals, choicest meats, and superior table service were provided. A wait staff of nearly 200 was required, which included, among others, 75 waiters, 7 cooks, and, according to Seneca Ray Stoddard, "the ladies who washed the dishes, etc." The hotel manager and groups of dining staff members often moved together between a prominent southern hotel in the winter and the Fort William Henry Hotel in the summer. The 16-foot-high pillared foyer and public area were decorated mostly in white and gold. The hotel offices, stagecoach and telegraph offices, and a relic cabinet were located in this area. (Stoddard; courtesy of the Crandall Public Library.)

Just after opening for the season, the first Fort William Henry Hotel burned to the ground in a spectacular fire on June 24, 1909. The owners, the Delaware and Hudson Company, made immediate plans to rebuild and, in 1911, the second Fort William Henry opened. It was smaller but more up-to-date, with private baths and other conveniences. It accommodated just 200 guests and, though luxurious, it was less ostentatious than its predecessor.

The new Fort William Henry Hotel featured an ornate cement and marble-columned pergola at the water's edge, which could be accessed from the hotel by terraced steps and an elegant archway over the beach road. Within the pergola were fabulous shops, a cafe with sweeping views of the lake, and a clubhouse. The clubhouse, known as a casino, had reading and game rooms and a dance floor, where the hotel orchestra played regularly.

The Sagamore Hotel was located a scenic 10-mile drive from Caldwell, along the winding west lakeshore—a road often traveled for fashionable afternoon drives. The Sagamore Tally-Ho pictured is on the Bolton-Green Island bridge near Wapanak, the cottage of E. Burgess Warren, a principal investor in the Sagamore Hotel. (Courtesy of Hugh Allen Wilson.)

Most Sagamore guests arrived and departed by steamboat since stagecoach transportation was limited. Parklike lawns with towering trees and flower-bordered walks led from the steamboat landing to the hotel. The Sagamore appealed to a clientele that preferred quiet elegance. (Stoddard; courtesy of The Chapman Historical Museum.)

A group of Philadelphia investors formed the Green Island Improvement Corporation to build a hotel on the island. The Sagamore opened on July 1, 1883. The exterior porticos, balconies, and gables were tinted in soft shades of rose and green, which harmonized well with the natural setting. The rooms were lavishly furnished, new Edison incandescent lighting was used throughout, and plumbing facilities were the best available at that time. Rates in 1888 were $4 per day and $17 to $25 per week, according to season. (Courtesy of Hugh Allen Wilson.)

On June 27, 1893, a fire that started in the hotel laundry consumed the entire rambling Sagamore structure. Only the artistically designed terra-cotta fireplaces remained as mute evidence of the former magnificence. Even though the building was not fully insured, the stockholders decided to rebuild immediately. (Courtesy of the Bolton Historical Museum.)

The second Sagamore opened in the summer of 1894. It was similar in design to the first, but during reconstruction many newer amenities were added, including private bathrooms and an electric elevator. Facilities for every imaginable activity were available, including a small golf course. Roswell P. Flower, governor of New York, is pictured at the right center visiting the Sagamore in 1894, shortly after its reopening. A.B. Colvin of Glens Falls stands at the left center. (Courtesy of Hugh A. Wilson.)

Fire struck the hotel a second time, destroying the Sagamore II in 1914. Less than half of the cost was covered by the insurance, and there was divided opinion among the investors regarding the wisdom of rebuilding. In addition to the financial considerations, land for the addition of an 18-hole golf course, which was considered necessary, was either unavailable or unsuitable. (Courtesy of the Bolton Historical Museum.)

John Boulton Simpson, a principal stockholder and president of the Green Island Improvement Company, is pictured in September 1906 at the steering wheel of his 50-horsepower Welsh automobile on the Sagamore grounds. Simpson's home was in New York City, where he was owner of the American Agency of the Estey Piano Company. At Lake George, he was a founding member and an officer of the Lake George Club and was influential in many social and civic activities. (Courtesy of Hugh Allen Wilson.)

Family and friends are pictured above in J.B. Simpson's six-cylinder, 60-horsepower Great Arrow. These individuals were part of the summer colony that used a temporary dining facility known as the Sagamore Annex for a number of years following the 1914 fire. Additional construction was delayed by many complications; however, in 1922, a new 100-room Sagamore Club House was finally opened and then expanded in 1929 and 1930. The third Sagamore Hotel continues to operate as a world-class resort. (Courtesy of Hugh Allen Wilson.)

The investors in the Green Island Improvement Company built four elegant summer cottages for themselves on Green Island in addition to the Sagamore Hotel. These cottages formed part of the famous Millionaires' Row. The opulent J.B. Simpson residence, known as Nirvana, is pictured above in 1896. The cone-shaped tower repeats the architectural style of the first Sagamore Hotel, which was built at the same time. Nirvana Farm on the mainland completed the land holdings of the estate. The yacht *Folly* is at the dock. (Courtesy of Hugh Allen Wilson.)

Many lodging options were available to the Lake George visitor. The accommodations varied in size, amenities, and ambiance, as well as price. A representative sampling has been selected to demonstrate the diversity and to show what one might expect to find at similar establishments along the lake. (Wooley.)

A number of lovely hotels enjoyed a loyal patronage from an affluent clientele who did not wish to be a part of the social whirl at the Fort William Henry or the Sagamore Hotels. The Marion was located on the west shore of the lake, adjoining the Lake George Club, where guests of the Marion had golf privileges. Steamers stopped at the dock four times a day, and within the hotel there were telephone and telegraph lines and a post office, which used the postmark "Westside." (Wooley.)

Marion House was built in the 1850s and expanded in 1888 to accommodate 400 guests. The guests were served meals in the dining room, pictured above *c.* 1909. Other amenities included an elevator, steam heat, and electric and gas lights. Rates in 1888 were $3.50 per day or $14 to $25 per week. In 1909, rates had increased to $18 to $39 per week. (Wooley.)

Almost all hotels of this size hired musicians for the summer to provide music several times a day and for a hop (as a dance was called) at least once a week. Guests here enjoyed the natural beauty of the area and a slightly more relaxed ambiance. Every facility for amusement was available. (Wooley.)

HOTEL MARION

Joseph H. Marvel

LAKE GEORGE, N. Y.

...DINNER...

GUMBO A LA CREOLE

CONSOMME VERMICELLI

GHERKINS

OLIVES

BOILED ROCKFISH PARSLEY SAUCE

POTATOES NATURAL

MACARONI A LA NEAPOLITAN

ROAST RIBS OF PRIME BEEF AU JUS

ROAST YOUNG CHICKEN BROWN GRAVY

MASHED POTATOES AND BOILED POTATOES

CREAMED SPINACH

SUGAR CORN

LETTUCE SALAD

FARINA PUDDING WINE SAUCE

VANILLA CUSTARD PIE

COFFEE ICE CREAM

ASSORTED CAKE

EDAM CHEESE

CRACKERS

COFFEE

ALL DISHES NOT ON BILL OF FARE WILL BE CHARGED EXTRA.
ALL SERVICE TO ROOM CHARGED EXTRA.

MEAL HOURS:

BREAKFAST 8 TO 9.30   LUNCHEON 1 TO 2.30   DINNER 6.30 TO 8.

WEDNESDAY,
AUGUST 11, 1909.

GUESTS ARE INVITED TO MAIL THIS MENU TO THEIR FRIENDS

The Hotel Marion advertised that its table was first-class in every respect and that its service was the best obtainable. Milk and cream came from the Marion herd of Jersey cows, and fresh vegetables were available in variety and abundance from the hotel farm. The advertisement also stressed pure, soft springwater.

Fresh produce, often from the hotel's own garden, required a great deal of daily preparation. Frequently, the waitresses were responsible for this chore, along with other duties such as housekeeping and laundry. Waitresses are pictured above preparing vegetables for the day at the Silver Bay Inn. (Courtesy of the Silver Bay Association.)

From the grand hotels to the most modest boardinghouses, laundry was generated in huge amounts. Tablecloths, napkins, sheets, pillowcases, towels, and personal articles all had to be dealt with, even in rainy weather. The Hillside Hotel laundry in Hague is pictured above. (Courtesy of the Clifton F. West Historical Museum.)

The amount of baggage that passed through Lake George during the course of a summer was staggering. Guests arrived for extended periods, often the entire summer, with steamer trunks that were filled with clothing suitable for many occasions. (Courtesy of the Silver Bay Association.)

Cottages and boardinghouses were often a five- or ten-minute walk from the steamer dock. Guidebooks mention the availability of a porter at some of the steamer docks to assist with the delivery of luggage. A wheelbarrow served many purposes. (Stoddard DETAIL; courtesy of The Chapman Historical Museum.)

The United States Hotel was one of the earliest to be built on the lake, c. 1850. It fell into financial difficulty when the nearby Fort William Henry Hotel was built in 1855 and former patrons of the United States Hotel moved on to the newer one. A school for young ladies at the site fared no better. The property was then purchased by Francis G. Crosby, who enlarged and improved the hotel and renamed it Crosbyside. Seneca Ray Stoddard likened the hotel to "a great home to which familiar faces come year after year." Hotel rates of $14 to $25 per week in the 1880s were similar to those of the Fort William Henry Hotel. An 1891 advertisement indicates that Crosbyside was still thriving, although under different ownership; however, around the beginning of the 20th century, the property was abandoned. In 1902, the property was purchased for back taxes by Spencer and Katrina Trask, perhaps best known for Yaddo, their estate in Saratoga Springs, which now serves as an artist retreat. (Stoddard; courtesy of the Crandall Public Library.)

In 1903, Spencer and Katrina Trask leased the former Crosby property to Mary Wiltsie Fuller rent free to assist her in providing an affordable vacation for women working in the textile and shirt factories of Troy and Cohoes. In 1907, the Trasks deeded the property to her to assure the continuation of the program. The large cottage of the Crosby family, built in the 1870s, is pictured c. 1880. It was renamed the Holiday House by the association now known as Wiawaka and serves as their main house. Following the death of Mary Wiltsie Fuller in 1943, the building became known as the Fuller House in recognition of her untiring humanitarian efforts on behalf of Wiawaka. (Stoddard; courtesy of The Chapman Historical Museum.)

Rose Cottage, a Crosby guest cottage dating to the 1870s, is another of the Victorian buildings deeded to Mary Wiltsie Fuller by Spencer and Katrina Trask. Additional property deeded by George Foster Peabody is also still in use; however, the old hotel was destroyed by fire in 1905.

The association took as its name the Native American word *wiawaka*, which implies "the spirit of God in woman." A Wiawaka brochure explains that the name expressed the hope of the founders that their work would be of the spirit, that rest and rejuvenation would be given, and that all within the Wiawaka circle would be uplifted. The facilities were originally created for the use of members of the Girls' Friendly Society of the St. Paul's Episcopal Church in Troy, NY. In 1907, the scope was broadened to include professional and self-supporting women of all denominations and, additionally, half-rate fares on the Delaware and Hudson Railroad were arranged so that guests might come from greater distances. Through the efforts of Mary Wiltsie Fuller and generous benefactors, the rate for room and board was $3.50 per week when the resort opened on July 4, 1903. Wiawaka women are pictured here at Holiday House, *c.* 1910. Today, the Wiawaka Holiday House Inc. continues its affordable policy as a nonprofit, nonsectarian retreat and educational center dedicated to enriching the lives of women and the preservation of the historic property. (Courtesy of the Wiawaka Holiday House Inc.)

Pictured on this page are two views from the early 1900s of the large, refurbished Wiawaka Holiday House living room. The room remains very much the same today, as do the remaining vintage Wiawaka buildings and the tranquil grounds. Together, they provide a glimpse, as if in a time warp, of an almost unaltered Lake George vacation resort with roots still in the 19th century.

Wiawaka is listed on the National and New York State Registers of Historic Sites. In addition to its gracious Victorian and Adirondack buildings, seven bateaux sunk in 1758 during the French and Indian War lay submerged in a Heritage Preserve off the Wiawaka boathouse. Affixed to a rock on the shore nearby is a 1921 plaque that commemorates the founding of the American Canoe Association.

Jabez Patchin built a one-room cabin on the present Silver Bay Association grounds in the early 1800s. The cabin was enlarged into a farmhouse by Seneca Prouty and, during the years 1885 to 1897, was expanded into a small hotel by Judge John J. Wilson. The Silver Bay Hotel reached its present recognizable form with the large addition built by Silas Paine at the beginning of the 20th century. Paine operated the hotel on a commercial basis for approximately two years but, in 1902, agreed to reserve its use for Christian conferences and missionary education. In 1904, he sold the property at half its value to those operating the conferences. That year, it was incorporated as the Silver Bay Association for Christian Conferences and Training. Leadership for the association came from the YMCA, the Young People's Missionary Movement, and various church and educational institutions. Since its inception, the association has served a varied constituency that includes numerous denominations as well as college, industrial, international, and military YMCA and YWCA groups. Through its extensive summer training

program for Y workers, Silver Bay Association began to be known as "the Summer Home of the YMCA." The view pictured above, c. 1910, shows the campus as seen on an approach from the steamer dock. The four-story hotel completed c. 1900 is in the right center. The rustic-style auditorium with bell tower, built in 1909, is in the left center. Five classrooms are seen on the far left. A city YWCA conference is pictured below. Today, the Silver Bay Association operates as a "YMCA Christian conference center serving individuals, families, and groups. Through its programs and activities, the Association seeks to strengthen the application of Christian principles, develop human potential, foster a concern for others and for the world in which we live, encourage a commitment for service, and offer opportunities for self-renewal for spiritual, mental and physical growth." The organization is approaching its 100th anniversary as a conference center. Thirty-two buildings on the campus are included on the National and New York State Historic Records. (Lower photograph courtesy of the Silver Bay Association.)

Forest Inn was built *c.* 1901 by Silas Paine. It provided additional and less expensive lodging to address the needs of varied constituencies visiting Silver Bay. The dormitory building with its elaborate split-log geometric half-timbering is an excellent example of rustic Adirondack-style architecture. Still in use, the building is now known as Hepbron Hall.

Originally built *c.* 1900 and subsequently enlarged, as shown above, the association's bathhouse is another wonderful example of traditional turn-of-the-century Adirondack architecture. It was used for changing clothing, since association rules did not permit bathing suits to be worn anywhere on campus, other than at the beach. An attendant was on duty to hang wet suits out to dry and to have them ready for the swimmer's next plunge. (Wooley.)

The Silver Bay Association boat dock is pictured here with its many boats, c. 1915. The steamer landing is seen in the background with a flag flying on the roof. The building's architecture is in the turn-of-the-century rustic Adirondack style. It was from this dock that the majority of the conferees arrived and departed. (Courtesy of the Silver Bay Association.)

Antoinette Carter Hughes, the mother of Helen Hughes, is pictured laying the cornerstone of the Helen Hughes Memorial Chapel at Silver Bay on June 19, 1921. The women in the background are Vassar classmates of Helen Hughes, who was a 1914 graduate. She devoted herself to YWCA work, serving as a member of the national board. After her death from influenza in 1920, Vassar alumnae and co-workers organized a drive for the construction of a chapel in her memory at Silver Bay. Her father served as the governor of New York, chief justice of the U.S. Supreme Court, and U.S. secretary of state, and also made an unsuccessful bid for the presidency. (Wooley; courtesy of the Silver Bay Association.)

The YMCA Summer School Physical Institute was one of the many conferences that used the Silver Bay Association facilities. Physical directors are pictured in front of the Fisher Gymnasium in 1926. The gym was constructed from 1916 to 1917 and was named for Dr. George J. Fisher, who served as the YMCA international secretary for physical education. Many physical directors learned to play basketball here at the hands of the game's creator, James Naismith of Springfield College. (Courtesy of the Silver Bay Association.)

The Silver Bay School for Boys was established under the auspices of the Silver Bay Association in 1918. The school was made possible through a generous gift from Silas and Mary Paine in memory of their son Harrington Spear Paine. Leading universities recognized the school's high scholastic standards; however, the Great Depression brought about the demise of the school in 1935. The 1920 student body is pictured above. (Courtesy of the Silver Bay Association.)

The boys' school offered a strong college preparatory program. The chemistry lab is pictured above. Additionally, emphasis was placed on religious instruction and practical education. Principles learned in the classroom were applied to work projects, such as the operation of a small sawmill, the construction of cabins and footbridges, ice harvesting, maple sugaring, soap making, and farm chores. (Courtesy of the Silver Bay Association.)

A woodcraft camp organized by Ernest Thompson-Seton was held at Silver Bay in 1910. Numerous boys' organizations were represented among the 125 attendees at the experimental encampment. Ideas formulated at the woodcraft camp led to the organization of the Boy Scouts of America later that year. Silver Bay is recognized as their first leadership training site. Known as Black Wolf, Thompson-Seton is standing to the right at the woodcraft camp, 1910. (Courtesy of the Silver Bay Association.)

Subsequent encampments for the training of scoutmasters of the Boy Scouts of America were held as part of the Silver Bay Summer Institute in 1911 and 1912. Daniel Carter Beard, national commissioner of the Boy Scouts of America, is pictured above, demonstrating "throwing the hatchet" in 1912. A Boy Scout council ring was dedicated at the site of the first encampment in 1947 and continues to be maintained. (Courtesy of the Silver Bay Association.)

Camp Iroquois at Glen Eyrie is representative of yet another vacation option that was available to Lake George visitors. The camp, which was located on the eastern shore south of Gull Bay, opened prior to 1910. The Adirondack twig work on the dock is representative of the rustic theme of the camp. Campers regularly gathered there for the arrival of the steamer, where an enthusiastic greeting was assured. (Courtesy of Brookside, SCHS.)

The steamer *Horicon* is pictured at the Glen Eyrie landing. Camp Iroquois was not a regularly scheduled stop, but steamboats docked there when signaled. The post office and store were located in the building at the right of the dock. (Wooley; Brookside, SCHS.)

Under the direction of George F. Tibbitts, interstate secretary of the YMCA of Washington, D.C., Camp Iroquois was originally opened to accommodate young men. Later, its focus shifted to young adults and families. The camp facilities included a mix of tents and bungalows. (Wooley.)

This Adirondack lean-to provided campers with a spot to gather around for campfires, songfests, and group activities. Campers also enjoyed waterfront activities, field sports, and hiking. There were a number of trails leading from the camp. One led to Manitou's Cliff, which afforded an awe-inspiring panoramic view of the lake. (Wooley.)

The breadline suggests that meals at Glen Eyrie were served buffet style and that dining was more informal than at other accommodations pictured in this book. Tablecloths may have been made of oilcloth, but despite the rustic nature of the camp, they were not overlooked. (Wooley; Brookside, SCHS.)

A Glen Eyrie postcard from "Aunt Lillian" enthusiastically announces that she is living in a tent and enjoys paddling in the nice clean water. On another postcard, "Helen" at Glen Eyrie reports that "This is the best vacation ever and an ideal spot to enjoy it." (Wooley; Brookside, SCHS.)

The Adirondack Camp for Boys, located on the northeast shore of Lake George, south of Blair's Bay, was established in 1904 by Dr. Elias G. Brown of New York City, who was a pioneer in the summer camp movement. Under his leadership, the camp stressed physical development in a rugged outdoor setting, as well as the development of initiative, self-reliance, cooperation, and courtesy. According to a Delaware and Hudson guidebook of the period, "The camp is known on Lake George and through the Adirondack region by the character of its boys—brown, rugged, skillful, happy, and refined." The 1912 picture above illustrates the all-woolen uniform that was designed to be suitable for camp conditions. It consisted of a dark blue sleeveless jersey (emblazoned with an A), short pants, and knee stockings. The boys, ranging in age from 10 to 16, came from socially prominent, affluent, New York City area families (for the most part) to "rough it" at the lake. In 1905, the cost for the entire summer was $150. (Wooley.)

Campers slept in tents accommodating seven boys and a leader. The tents were opened to sunshine and breeze, but heavy canvas flies and raised-board floors afforded some protection during inclement weather. Sports facilities were provided for tennis, basketball, volleyball, baseball, archery, and rifle shooting. A stable and provisions for other activities were also included. (Wooley.)

Food was prepared by professional cooks and served by counselors-in-training. Other staff included experienced woodsmen, educators, coaches, and college men, many of whom had been former Adirondack campers. The boys received instruction in practical camping, woodcraft, and nature study. (Wooley.)

The Deep Swim, Adirondack Camp.
Glenburnie-on-Lake George, N.Y.

Water sports were among the most popular of the camp activities. There were two swimming areas. "The Cove," located along the shoreline, had a sand beach with a pier and rafts for the junior swimmers. The "Senior Swim," located in deeper water, is pictured above. Camp swimming instruction almost guaranteed that all campers would know how to swim well by the end of the season. (Wooley.)

The Canoe Fleet at
Adirondack Camp
2104

The ability to handle a canoe and swim was required for many of the favorite camp trips. Instruction in the tireless long-distance stroke of the voyageur was stressed. The "fleet" included Adirondack guideboats, flat-bottom junior rowboats, 17-foot Old Town canoes, and 30-foot war canoes. All were in constant use by the campers. (Wooley.)

Trips throughout the region were an essential part of the summer experience. Mountain climbing and canoe expeditions ranged from simple one- or two-day trips to two-week wilderness adventures. Adirondack campers are seen above, boarding the train at Port Kent en route to Ausable Chasm in 1909. In cooler weather, a wool flannel shirt, a heavy dark blue V-neck sweater (with the emblazoned A), and knickers with woolen stockings replaced the sleeveless uniform.

The flag-raising ceremony pictured here is *c*. 1912. Today, Camp Adirondack operates as a coed facility. The haunting bugle call still echoes over the camp for evening taps. (Wooley.)

Four

Bays and Byways

The area that we now call the Village and the Town of Lake George was previously known as Caldwell. The name that was historically correct at the time has been used throughout the book. Caldwell, at the southern end of the lake, was the point of departure for many lake excursions. This chapter explores the lake's picturesque bays and interesting byways for a glimpse of the sights seen by those making the trip from Caldwell to Ticonderoga many years ago. Pictured is the view north from the Fort William Henry Hotel grounds, showing the fountain and gazing ball in the foreground. (Stoddard.)

The town of Caldwell was formed in 1810 and was known by that name until 1962. The location of the village that developed at the head of the lake contributed to Caldwell's growth as a tourist center. In 1903, it was incorporated as the Village of Lake George within the town of Caldwell, producing some confusion when speaking of the "town." In 1962, the town of Caldwell officially changed its name to the Town of Lake George.

This early view of the Caldwell waterfront illustrates the peaceful setting that existed c. 1870. As additional docks and stagecoach and rail lines were located adjacent to the Fort William Henry Hotel, tourism increased dramatically. In 1875, approximately 15,000 guests arrived or passed through this hub; by 1890, the number was 100,000. Many stayed for extended periods of time. Gradually, the tranquility was replaced by tourist activity and commercial interests that catered to the tourists' needs. (Stoddard; courtesy of the Crandall Public Library.)

The Trout Pavilion at Kattskill Bay was known as a fishing resort but also had a billiard room, bowling alley, lawn tennis court, and croquet lawn. The *Lake George Mirror* of June 20, 1891, reported that "A more delightful spot could not well be imagined. It is a veritable haven of rest for the tired man of business, and, with all, does not exclude the opportunity for social enjoyment." A farm connected with the facility supplied the dining room with fresh vegetables. The Trout Pavilion was owned by the Cronkhite family for the majority of its existence. (Stoddard; courtesy of The Chapman Historical Museum.)

The Kattskill House stood in a grove of trees on a terraced bank overlooking Kattskill Bay, with an extensive view of the lake beyond. Attractive benches and lawn swings, potted plants, and foliage provided a restful setting. A noted fishing ground was located one mile from the house, and the hotel's fleet of rowboats was in constant use. The Kattskill House burned in August 1908.

The Lake George Club, located on the west shore south of the Marion House, was formally organized and incorporated on November 16, 1908, by prominent members of the Lake George community to enhance the social life of the lake. The club, often called "The Millionaires' Club," opened on August 14, 1909, providing its members with an anchorage for their boats, a golf course, tennis courts, and a clubhouse with dining facilities. (Wooley.)

The "Great and the Gracious" were a moving force behind the Lake George Club. Spencer Trask, the club's first president, and George Peabody were particularly involved in its planning. The list of founding members reads like a list of Who's Who, including Bixby, Broesel, Cramer, Knapp, Meyer, three Peabodys, Reis, Simpson, Warren, and Watrous. (Wooley.)

Pictured here in 1889, the Lake View House, located on Bolton Bay, was built in the early 1870s. Seneca Ray Stoddard made a particular point of mentioning the picturesque rows of trees and that every effort had been made "to leave nature's perfect work comparatively untouched while . . . making all trim and accessible." This was at a time when many lots had been clear-cut for lumber and fuel. An unusual feature he mentioned in the early 1900s was a darkroom for the convenience of amateur photographers. Transportation to the public dock at Bolton Landing was provided by a small steamboat or carriage. The July 4, 1902 *Lake George Mirror* reported that "Every evening, in the large and spacious music hall, the guests gather and while (*sic*) away their time to the soft music. Another perfectly up-to-date and enjoyable pastime is ping pong." (Stoddard; courtesy of The Chapman Historical Museum.)

Bolton was originally part of the large territory of Thurman, which included most of Warren County. The Town of Bolton was organized on March 25, 1799, and its first town meeting was held on April 2, 1799, making it the oldest of the lake towns. At the time of its incorporation, Bolton included Hague and parts of Caldwell and Horicon. More than half of the islands of Lake George are located within its boundaries; it includes more shoreline than any other town. One of the many year-round activities supported by the community was the Bolton Band, pictured here c. 1905. (Courtesy of the Bolton Historical Museum.)

Bolton's first school was built c. 1800 on top of Federal Hill. Six more school districts were established by 1810 and, eventually, there were ten. The District Eight School on the road to Trout Lake is pictured above. A four-room brick schoolhouse was built c. 1898 where instruction included a two-year high school program. In 1928, all schools were centralized and the present high school was built. (Courtesy of the Bolton Historical Museum.)

The lake steamboats made regularly scheduled stops; however, additional service was available at other docks upon signal from the shore. The man pictured at the left is waving the flag, requesting the steamer to stop at the Mohican House dock in Bolton Landing. The property was sold at the beginning of the 20th century to William Bixby of St. Louis, Missouri. Bixby was president of the American Car and Foundry Company. It was on this property that Bixby built his stately mansion, Mohican Point. (Courtesy of the Bolton Historical Museum.)

George O. Knapp, co-founder of the Union Carbide Corporation, built an impressive estate on a ledge of Shelving Rock 200 feet above the lake in 1902. The site chosen had a superb view of the entire Narrows and broad sweeps of the lake to the south and north. A unique feature was the construction of an electric cable car to transport people and freight from the boathouse directly into the basement of the mansion. In 1917, a short circuit in the mechanism started a fire that could not be stopped, and the house and its contents were totally lost. The mansion was not rebuilt. Knapp's yacht, the *Sayonara*, is seen at the right. (Wooley.)

Italian Garden
of Mr. Knapp
Shelving Rock, Lake George N.Y.

The Knapp estate included a formal garden. It was located below the massive retaining walls that permitted the home to be constructed on a small ledge of Shelving Rock. The garden was terraced into the rocky embankment and included a stone-pillared colonnade. Native trees, ferns, and moss-covered rock provided a backdrop. (Wooley.)

The One Hundred Island House was opened in 1875 at the base of Shelving Rock. The hotel was one of several located on the east shore in the isolated section of the Narrows. Removed from other forms of entertainment, masquerades and hilarious costumed parades of ingenious outfits provided occasional social amusement. George Knapp purchased the property in 1894 and summered there until his imposing estate was built on the mountainside. The hotel was dismantled in 1905. (Courtesy of the Crandall Public Library.)

Paradise Bay is perhaps the loveliest and certainly the best known of the lake's many picturesque bays. It was purchased by George Knapp in 1904 and became part of his accumulated land holdings—holdings that included 3,500 acres and 6 or more miles of shoreline from Shelving Rock Bay to Black Mountain Point. Most of the holdings were acquired by New York State in 1941 for public use.

Lakeside Cottage was built on the lake's east shore, north of Black Mountain, in the late 1870s. The quaint Victorian cottage continues to be a familiar Huletts' landmark. (Wooley.)

Gaiety and merriment prevailed at Huletts. Seneca Ray Stoddard wrote in 1909, "Amusements are hunting and fishing with dancing almost every evening. It is said there are no dull days at Huletts, which, no doubt, comes very near the truth as the proprietor caters to the fads and fancies of young people, and they seem to appreciate it to full value, making his life a joyful burden at times." Henry W. Buckle acquired the property in 1898 and sold it to William Wyatt in 1913. Two years later, the old Hulett House, seen here, burned, but a new Hulett House opened the next season. (Courtesy of the Bolton Historical Museum.)

ACK MT. FROM "BARTLETTS" LAKE GEORGE

Windmills provided a practical source of power for pumping water and driving generators. The windmill was usually mounted on a tower 20 feet or more above surrounding structures to get the full force of the wind. The Bartlett House windmill, pictured here, took advantage of the prevailing breeze that blew along the lake. The view looks south toward the northern end of the Narrows and Black Mountain. (Wooley.)

Overlooking Divinity Bay and Sabbath Day Point, the Bartlett House was one of several boardinghouses nestled under the shadow of Bloomer Mountain. The house was able to entertain about 25 summer boarders and typified the smaller boardinghouses that were prevalent up and down the lake.

Graciousness was not limited to the larger hotels, and the size of the accommodation was not an indicator of a good meal. Proprietors of smaller establishments prided themselves on food that was well prepared and properly served.

Sabbath Day Point, located on the west shore, provided a convenient resting place for Native Americans and for the armies of the Colonial and Revolutionary Wars as they traveled the water highway. Its gentle shoreline and flat terrain were more inviting than the heavily timbered, steep-sided mountain shoreline found around most of the lake. The steamer *Sagamore* is pictured making a stop at the Sabbath Day Point dock. (Wooley.)

Native Americans used the area over which these young people are walking, *c.* 1910, as a campsite. British Gen. James Abercromby's army of over 15,000 in 1758 and Gen. Jeffrey Amherst's army of 11,000 the following year also encamped here on their way to Fort Ticonderoga. Gen. Henry Knox passed through on his way to Boston in December 1775 with the cannons from Fort Ticonderoga. (Wooley.)

Samuel Adams provided accommodations for Lake George travelers at Sabbath Day Point during the 1760s. Later, Samuel Westurn enlarged his farmhouse, which was known as the Sabbath Day Point House, to accommodate 25 guests. The property was further expanded by Frank Carney, and he and later his family continued to operate Sabbath Day Point House from the late 1880s until 1957. A farm of 450 acres provided fresh vegetables, butter, cream, and eggs. Bathing, tennis, croquet, baseball, boating, fishing, and hunting were advertised as being available. (Wooley.)

Grace Memorial Union Chapel, located at the northern end of Sabbath Day Point, was organized as a nondenominational place of worship on August 11, 1884. Plans for the building were donated by William B. Tuttle, a well-known New York architect and the designer of Carnegie Hall. The chapel is an early example of precut framing. Placed on the New York State and National Registers of Historic Places in 1982, the chapel continues to hold Sunday services during the summer months. (Wooley.)

The lake's many islands have been popular camping sites over the years. In 1880, Seneca Ray Stoddard reported, "During July and August, Lake George teems with nomadic life . . . and vagrant communities appear and disappear as if by magic; white tents gleam among the dark green foliage . . ." Camping equipment was advertised for rent by the week or season. The delivery, setup, and removal of complete camping outfits were also offered. Campers are pictured here on Delaware Island. (Wooley; Brookside, SCHS.)

The launch *Mohawk* is depicted here *c.* 1907 near the Delaware Island campsites pictured above. This family enjoys one of the most popular activities on the lake. Delaware Island is located near Uncas Hotel between Sabbath Day Point and Silver Bay.

Smith Sexton built Hotel Uncas c. 1890 on the west shore of Lake George, where, according to the novel *The Last of the Mohicans*, Uncas landed and fled from the pursuing Native Americans to the cliffs above. A wedding party is pictured leaving from the hotel's exceptionally long steamer dock, which measured 255 feet. It was probably the longest on the lake. The hotel was briefly known as Hawkeye Inn; today, it continues as Northern Lake George Resort. (Wooley.)

Silas Paine built an imposing three-story summer home on his Silver Bay estate, *c.* 1895. The residence was complete with wide, surrounding porches and a Queen Ann-style tower, which featured scalloped trim. The observatory, pictured here, is a prominent landmark at the water's edge. Silas Paine, described as a naturalist, industrialist, and philanthropist, rose to the upper ranks of Standard Oil in the employment of John D. Rockefeller Jr. (Wooley.)

The lovely Oneita Bay, also known as Van Buren Bay, is seen in this view from the stone gateway to Silas and Mary Paine's estate, just north of the Silver Bay Hotel. The winding stone-walled road that passes the property leads north to Hague. (Wooley.)

Across the lake on the east shore and a little farther north, Gull Bay dips in and around the shoreline, forming lovely multiple bays. Still farther north on the east shore, Blair's Bay and the Glenburnie Club are located near the rocky promontory of Anthony's Nose. (Wooley; Brookside, SCHS.)

The first schoolhouse in Hague was a log structure located near the present Hague cemetery. Five other districts were eventually established. The Hague South District schoolhouse, shown above, was located near the intersection of Split Rock Road and the present Route 9N between Silver Bay and Hague. All school districts were consolidated in 1926. (Courtesy of the Clifton F. West Historical Museum.)

This steamer dock was the usual point of arrival at Hague. Hague, which had separated from Bolton on April 6, 1807, was first known as Rochester; however, a year later, the name Hague was adopted. Brooks and streams in the area furnished power for saw and gristmills between the 1830s and early 1900s. Lumbering and graphite mining were also prosperous enterprises for the community. (Wooley.)

The 30-passenger launch *Uncas* is pictured above at the Hague Village corner. The *Uncas* was built by Jesse Sexton and launched at Hague in 1910. Six teams of horses were required to move the boat from his shop to the lake. The Hillside Hotel is seen in the center background. The village bowling alley is at the left. (Courtesy of the Clifton F. West Historical Museum.)

Hague was a thriving lake community through the 1920s. A half-dozen good hotels dotted the shoreline. Altogether the Phoenix Hotel, Hillside, Iroquois, Trout House, Rising House, and Island Harbor House were able to accommodate over 400 guests. Guidebooks described the town as peaceful and stated that "excellent fishing grounds were at hand." The June 20, 1891 *Lake George Mirror* reported that over 2,000 pounds of trout were taken that spring by guests at the Hillside and Island Harbor Houses. (Wooley.)

The Trout House started as a boardinghouse in the 1860s and was gradually expanded to the facility pictured here *c.* 1908. The Trout House was well known for its trout dinners and people came from all around the lake to enjoy them. In addition to the tennis court in front, croquet grounds were located on the plateau behind the house. The building burned in 1918 and was replaced by a second hotel, which was subsequently torn down; it was later replaced by a multiunit resort.

The Hague summer cottage of Harry Watrous, built in the early 1890s, is pictured above. Watrous, a well-known painter, was a founding member of the Lake George Club and the perpetrator of the Lake George Monster Hoax in 1904. Watrous and his neighbor Colonel Mann were competitive fishermen. After Mann tried to impress Watrous with a large artificial trout, Watrous created a "monster" controlled by pulleys. The "monster" broke the water's surface near Mann's boat, startling him and creating a sensational panic. (Wooley.)

The final view of our trip along the bays and byways of Lake George looks toward Heart Bay and the northern outlet of the lake. Pictured in the foreground is the Rogers Rock Hotel, which was built in 1874. Guests bought the hotel from the owner in 1903 and formed the Rogers Rock Club. Sloane Wilson, author of *All the Best People*, summered there as a boy. Some sources have reported that the hotel was torn down in 1948; however, evidence suggests that the actual year was 1942. (Wooley.)

Five

EXCURSIONS
AND DIVERSIONS

The lake, then as now, was best appreciated from the water. An excursion through the lake by steamboat was usually placed at the top of the visitor's list of things to do. By 1870, several guidebooks were available to enhance the trip by providing a running commentary on the points of interest seen along the way and the events that had taken place. Steamboat captains also added interesting narration. Various options were available on this popular one-day trip that permitted excursionists to visit Fort Ticonderoga or Lake Champlain.

Most visitors to Fort Ticonderoga arrived by horse and wagon from the Baldwin or Montcalm boat landings. For a number of years, travelers were able to obtain meals or overnight lodging at the Fort Ticonderoga Hotel, located on the grounds of the old fort, before returning to the steamer docks to continue their journey.

Even before its restoration, Fort Ticonderoga was a popular destination. The fort's ruins seemed to entice the historically inclined. In 1800, Abigail May wrote the following of her feelings in her diary, as recorded by Russell Bellico in the *Chronicles of Lake George:* "I paced over the stones awe struck . . . a cold chill ran through my veins . . . everything makes this spot teem with melancholy reflections—I knew not how to leave it, and ascended the wagon with regret—I should like to pass a day there alone." (Wooley.)

A picnic trip to the top of Prospect Mountain to enjoy the view was another popular day's outing. There was a 1.75-mile hiking trail, though the trip was commonly made by horse and wagon. In 1895, the 1.4-mile Otis Incline Railway was built up the mountainside. It was the longest and steepest cable railway constructed at that time, with a vertical rise of 1,600 feet. Two open cars carrying 60 passengers each operated every 30 minutes during the day and evening in the summer months. The cost for the exciting eight- to ten-minute ride was 50¢ for a round-trip. The railway carried over 5,000 passengers the first week of its operation. One passenger writing of his trip on a postcard described the ride as "scary." The Prospect Mountain House provided meals, dancing, and overnight accommodations at the top. Enthusiasm for the railway declined, and it ceased operation in 1903. The property was acquired by George Foster Peabody and donated to the State of New York. A toll road now operates to the top.

Many famous 19th-century writers and painters drew upon the picturesque scenery of the Lake George region and its equally compelling history for their artistic inspiration, as well as their subject matter. Images conjured in the mind by James Fenimore Cooper's *The Last of the Mohicans* (1826) and by the romantic paintings of the lake by the Hudson River School contributed to the growth of Lake George tourism in the latter half of the century. Visitors who were artistically inclined were anxious to capture the beauty of the lake themselves. The amateur interest in art that was prevalent around the lake is reflected in Seneca Ray Stoddard's 1882 photograph of the Horicon Sketching Club. (Stoddard; courtesy of The Chapman Historical Museum.)

Croquet was such a popular outdoor activity of the period that most accommodations, large or small, provided facilities for the sport and advertised their availability. In an 1891 description of the Marion House, croquet was referred to as the "old time favorite." The Marion House claimed that beautiful grounds and all the requirements were at hand. Seneca Ray Stoddard's *c.* 1875 croquet scene records the popular sport and the fashionable elegance found at many Lake George resorts during the latter part of the 19th century. (Stoddard; courtesy of The Chapman Historical Museum.)

Tug-of-war was one of the standard events scheduled for any field day or group outing in which members participated in races and games. It is hard to believe that any were more daintily dressed for the sport than the little ones appearing here on the Crosbyside lawn. This 1880 Seneca Ray Stoddard photograph also shows the elegant fashion seen in the croquet image at the top of the page. (Stoddard; courtesy of The Chapman Historical Museum.)

The Waltonians is the name taken by a group of Glens Falls sportsmen who formed a club in 1853, giving homage to the English author Izaak Walton (1593 to 1683). This club was formed on the 200th anniversary of the publication of Izaak Walton's classic on fishing, *The Compleat Angler or the Contemplative Man's Recreation* (1653). In 1855, the club made the first of 15 annual two-week camping excursions to Waltonian Isle near Hague. This very early encampment helped to popularize the lure of camping on the islands for which Lake George has become well known. The Waltonian camping trips were legendary and the luxury of their large

tents made "roughing it" a relative term. Each year, the group issued formal printed invitations to join them at their campsite for two days. One year's invitation included, "In Memory Lt. Charles Cushing, Founder of the Waltonians, Killed at Battle of Antietam 1862." The group pictured above displays items representative of the activities in which they were engaged during the August 18 to 19, 1869 "open tent." Additionally, there were receptions and dinners for which the Waltonians were well known. Club records suggest that the initial focus on fishing may have been eclipsed by spirited hilarity. (Stoddard; courtesy of the Crandall Public Library.)

The flamboyant Waltonian camping tradition continued to evolve for a number of years on Phelps (Mohican) Island in the Narrows after a fire burned the Waltonian Isle campsite in 1870. Uniforms such as those shown above added to the group's mystique. From their Phelps headquarters, the Waltonians made frequent trips to Fourteen Mile Island, where their presence enlivened the hotel's social scene. (Stoddard; courtesy of the Crandall Public Library.)

It is uncertain when the Waltonian tents vanished from Phelps (Mohican) Island, but Seneca Ray Stoddard photographed H. Colvin's rustic cabin on the island in 1884. In 1885, the New York State "forever wild" conservation law was passed. This law prohibited the practice of leasing state islands for personal use. Individuals with investments in property on state islands were permitted to remain as custodians until 1915, when illegal occupancy became an issue and the remaining cottages and camps were removed by the owners or the state. (Courtesy of the Crandall Public Library.)

The Glens Falls Club, founded March 8, 1887, was first known as the Glens Falls Athletic Association. Its name was officially changed in 1892 when the organization moved its headquarters to the Peck Building at Ridge and Glen Streets. The club membership roster included many of Glens Falls leading citizens. In 1903, the club rooms and main floor were renovated at considerable expense. In 1907, the club acquired a Lake George country house located at the site of the former Lake House. According to club records, the winter banquet and the Lake George outing and clambake were the highlights of the year. Both were "on a most elaborate scale . . . with no expense or trouble spared." The club picture above was taken the day of the clambake, *c.* 1909. When the club disbanded a few years later, the Elks took over the club's city facility and the memberships merged. (Courtesy of the Crandall Public Library.)

On August 3, 1880, the founding members of the American Canoe Association met on one of a small group of islands at Lake George, now known as the Canoe Islands, to unite "into one brotherhood the amateur canoeists of Canada and the United States." Their objective, as reported by Seneca Ray Stoddard, who was a member and the official photographer of the organization, was "to elevate the gentlemanly pastime of canoeing." Members attending the ACA annual meeting in 1882 are seen on the Crosbyside lawn. (Stoddard; courtesy of the Hillview Free Library.)

The American Canoe Association held its annual meeting at Lake George in 1881 and 1882. Regatta races off the Crosbyside shoreline were featured events. Note that the 1882 race pictured involves canoes outfitted with sails, which were known as sailing canoes. In 1921, the ACA placed a plaque at the Crosbyside site, now known as Wiawaka, commemorating the founding of the organization. (Stoddard; courtesy of the Hillview Free Library.)

An axe usually headed the list of items Seneca Ray Stoddard advised campers to have available. One is pictured in use, as the campers busy themselves with chores on Odell Island. There were no restrictions against cutting brush or trees on the islands at that time, but as camping became increasingly popular, various regulations were introduced to preserve the islands.

In addition to Odell's use as a camping and picnic site, the island provided a picturesque setting for the wedding ceremony at right. Canoe-shaped invitations with small birch bark paddles invited guests to Odell Island to celebrate the occasion on August 27, 1915. The numerous wedding attendants were joined by a long chain of goldenrod draped from one to another. (Courtesy of the Silver Bay Association.)

John Boulton Simpson was famous for hosting fabulous picnics and outings. Pictured above is a group of his wait staff on the Sagamore Hotel service dock, preparing to embark with supplies for an affair to be held at a picturesque point along the lake. Note the many baskets, crates, tubs, trays, sawhorses to set up tables, and china punch or chowder bowls. (Courtesy of Hugh Allen Wilson.)

In contrast to the simplicity of the activities on the preceding page, the notion of "roughing it" for these gentlemen was not only civilized but also sumptuous. J.B. Simpson is at the head of the table, c. 1894. Note the variety of the hats worn. (Courtesy of Hugh Allen Wilson.)

Simpson's yacht, the *Fanita*, was a showstopper by any standard. It was the most palatial as well as the fastest private yacht on the lake until the arrival of the *Ellide*. The *Fanita*, named after Simpson's daughter Fanny, was launched in 1890 and immediately figured prominently in the Lake George social scene. Pictured above, the *Fanita* is decked out for the 1891 Lake George Carnival held in Caldwell. (Courtesy of Hugh Allen Wilson.)

The *Fanita* was renowned for its luxury and Simpson entertained aboard with a frequency and an elegance that the "Great and Gracious" took for granted. The interior was handsomely finished with wood paneling and red leather seating. Formal red velvet draperies hung at the windows. Any invitation issued to view a regatta aboard the *Fanita* was gratefully received and formally accepted. (Courtesy of the Bolton Historical Museum.)

The sloping lawns of the Sagamore Hotel grounds provided spectators with an excellent view of regatta activity on the broad expanse of water off the shore of Green Island. The cedar rowboats with the distinctive wineglass-shaped stern, pictured in the foreground, were built in Bolton by Fred Smith, one of the master boat builders on Lake George. (Courtesy of Hugh Allen Wilson.)

A second view of the Sagamore grounds and regatta site is shown above. The Sagamore Regatta program (right) of August 25, 1898, lists competitions that were typical at most regattas of the period. The launch races involved steam-powered craft. The first official gasoline-powered race on the lake did not take place until 1906. Of course, private owners lost no time testing their own "play toys" against every new powerboat that arrived on the lake, and would replace their own by the next summer if it did not measure up. (Courtesy of the Bolton Historical Museum.)

Official Program

Sagamore Regatta

Thursday, August 25, 1898.

RACES COMMENCE AT 11 A. M.

THE FOLLOWING RACES WILL BE CONTESTED:

GENTLEMEN'S DOUBLES.

LADIES' DOUBLES.

BOYS' DOUBLES.

LIMITED TO BOYS 16 YEARS OLD.

GENTLEMEN'S SINGLES.

BOYS' SINGLES.

LADIES' AND GENTLEMEN'S DOUBLES.

LAUNCH RACE.

BOATMEN'S DOUBLES,

TUB RACE.

SWIMMING RACE.

Price 10 Cents.

BOATMEN'S SINGLES.

Regattas were an eagerly anticipated part of the summer social as well as boating scene. Numerous groups hosted well-attended events up and down the lake. Regattas at the head of the lake, held as early as 1879, took place in front of the Fort William Henry Hotel. At the northern end of the lake, well-known regattas were hosted by the Hague Rowing Association. The 12th annual Hague Regatta, on August 17, 1899, was an all-day affair. Rowing, canoe sailing, and launch races were contested. The men's free-for-all singles and doubles events were open to all men of the Lake George and Adirondack region. During the afternoon, E. Burgess Warren exhibited his steam yacht *Ellide* in a speed demonstration over a one-mile course. The Ticonderoga City Band was in attendance, and dinners were available that day at any of the hotels in town. The regatta hop was held at the Trout House that evening, and prizes were distributed.

Spectators and participants mingle at the annual Hague Regatta, which was hosted by the Hague Rowing Association, one of the first watersport clubs in the country.

E. Burgess Warren's *Ellide* is pictured in regatta dress. The *Ellide*, built in 1897, was the fastest boat in the world, and held the speed record of 40 miles per hour until 1902. (Courtesy of Hugh Allen Wilson.)

Launches *Fanita*, owned by John B. Simpson, and *Winnish*, owned by LeGrand C. Cramer, are pictured at a Hague Regatta, c. 1908. (Wooley.)

Count Casimer Mankowski in his boat *Ankle Deep* won the prestigious American Power Boat Association's Gold Challenge Cup Races on the St. Lawrence River in 1913. This permitted him to request that the event be held at Lake George the following year. For three days, huge crowds thronged the shoreline to view the 1914 races off Green Island. On the Sagamore grounds, the grandstand and box seats were taxed to capacity, and on the lake, spectators filled the decks of the *Horicon* and other small craft which were anchored in a roped-off area within the racecourse. (Wooley; courtesy of the Bolton Historical Museum.)

The 90-nautical-mile endurance race was run in three heats of five laps each around a 6-nautical-mile elliptical course laid out between markers near Dome Island and Montcalm Point. Scores were calculated on the basis of all three heats. Adversity struck the *Ankle Deep* during the third heat when its propeller shaft snapped; the Gold Cup defender placed a disappointing third. The reviewing stand on the Sagamore grounds is pictured above. (Courtesy of the Bolton Historical Museum.)

Baby Speed Demon II was the winner of the 1914 Gold Cup Race, as well as the short distance speed race. It set a new world's record of 50.49 miles per hour. (Wooley; Brookside, SCHS.)

Ankle Deep (left) is pictured with two other contenders, the *PDQ IV* and the *PDQ V*; the *Horicon* is in the background. (Wooley; Brookside, SCHS.)

Ankle Deep, the local favorite, failed to defend the Gold Cup title. Lake George had to wait beyond the time frame of this book for that honor. George Reis in *Lagarto* (the lizard) successfully defended his Gold Cup title in 1934 and 1935. (Wooley; Brookside, SCHS.)

In 1847, the game of lawn tennis was brought to the United States from Great Britain and caught on quickly. Hotels of all sizes provided courts for enthusiastic players. Tournaments were extremely popular with the ladies as well as the men and, despite ankle-length skirts, there were many excellent women players. Pictured above is the final mixed-doubles match during the Missionary Education Movement Conference in 1913. (Courtesy of the Silver Bay Association.)

The latest fashions were worn for this ladies' softball game. The batter's cap is unique. (Courtesy of the Silver Bay Association.)

Seneca Ray Stoddard gives this advice: "Ladies, wear what you have a mind to, you will anyway, but let me respectfully suggest that it be flannel next to you, with good strong shoes under foot, and a man's felt hat over head—take the man along, too, if you want to, he will be useful to row you about, take the fish off your hook, . . . etc." Actually, Flora Sexton, above, was a very capable individual who really did not need any help! (Courtesy of the Clifton F. West Historical Museum.)

Hiking was a popular activity for both men and women. The men in this view are headed out on an overnight trip with bedrolls, lanterns, and a traditional Adirondack pack basket. Rules of etiquette were more relaxed for the women, and some wore "short" mountain skirts with hems above the ankles. (Wooley.)

The old adage that "a picture is worth a thousand words" aptly applies to bathing suits of the early 1900s. While the concept of recreational bathing demonstrated a progressive approach to the 20th century, the bathing attire itself made definite concessions to strict 19th-century Victorian attitudes, which seem almost comical today.

Swimming became very popular once the idea took hold; however, walking around in bathing suits was not accepted. A bathhouse for changing in and out of proper clothing usually was not far from water's edge. (Courtesy of the Bolton Historical Museum.)

Advanced swimming skills were required to reach this deep-water raft located on the Silver Bay Association waterfront. The trench coat-like outfits on the adventurous young ladies pictured here c. 1911 would certainly have made the swim out to the raft more difficult. (Wooley; courtesy of the Silver Bay Association.)

This intrepid young lady challenges the norm with her avant-garde behavior. The heavy wet bathing suit seems to defy the law of gravity. (Wooley; courtesy of Silver Bay Association.)

The Lake George $10,000 Swiming Marathon – Boo

The Lake George American Legion sponsored the Lake George Marathon Swim, with the expectation that its members would raise the $10,000 prize set for the event. The goal fell far short, although the excitement did not. Boxing champion Jack Dempsey officially started the race from the Trout House beach in Hague on July 12, 1927, at 8:45 a.m. Regulations required each swimmer to be accompanied by a boat carrying a rower, a trainer, and a race official. More than 100 men and women swimmers registered for the international event, including champions from the United States, Norway, Canada, Germany, England, Belgium, and France. There was a question of whether the 28-mile distance could be completed because of the temperature of the water—despite the fact that a number of swimmers had already conquered

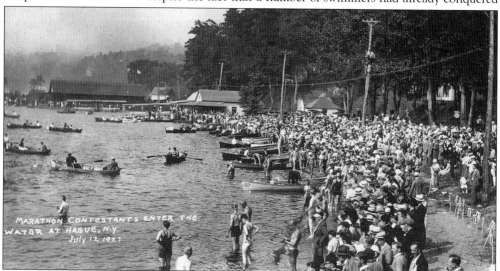

MARATHON CONTESTANTS ENTER THE WATER AT HAGUE, N.Y. July 12, 1927

Swimers About to Enter Water at Hague.

the English Channel. Swimmers struggled against wind and whitecaps; some developed cramps and other ailments; others tired and gave up along the way; still others were taken aboard the hospital boat, exhausted, one unconscious. Hours later, in the darkness, one swimmer lost contact with her boat and swam far off course before being located. Eventually, she gave up one mile short of the finish and placed second. Nineteen hours and 47 minutes after starting, Edward F. Keating of New York City emerged from the water at 4:32 a.m. at the Fort William Henry Pergola amidst flares, sirens, and a cheering crowd. The lone swimmer to complete the marathon received a purse of only $3,000!

Winter at Lake George must not be overlooked. In its frozen state, the lake offers additional opportunities for exciting seasonal activities. The large toboggan run pictured was built as an attraction for the initial winter opening of the Fort William Henry Hotel in 1914. The hotel was only successful as a year-round facility for a few years.

Ice-harness racing attracted enthusiastic crowds, occasionally numbering up to 800. The horses were sharp shod with four pointed metal calks on each shoe to prevent slipping. Hotly contested races were run on a kite-shaped track in front of the Fort William Henry Hotel and in Hague, where in February 1912, approximately 25 horses were stabled for a three-day series. Purses for the winners ranged from five bushels of oats to monetary awards of $25 to over $100. (Courtesy of the Crandall Public Library.)

Skating enthusiasts found veritable thrills in sail skating, which requires snow-free or black ice. Speeds of 30 to 48 miles per hour were reached on the skates. Maneuvering with the wind challenged both strength and coordination. Wind and cold challenged endurance. (Courtesy of the Bolton Historical Museum.)

When snow covered the surface of the ice, skaters switched to skis. Iceboating and iceboat racing were also popular. In addition to their sporting value, iceboats also provided a means of winter transportation. (Courtesy of the Bolton Historical Museum.)

Before the days of mechanical refrigeration, ice was harvested from the lake in winter and stored for summer use. To harvest the ice, snow was scrapped from the surface and the ice was marked for cutting by a horse-drawn ice plow. The teeth of the plow scored the ice into squares, and then the ice was sawed into blocks, using the grooves as guides. The ice needed to be at least 12 inches thick before it could be harvested, although 20 inches was generally preferred. (Courtesy of the Bolton Historical Museum.)

The blocks were floated to shore in a channel cut through the ice or transported by horse and sled to be stored in an icehouse. The blocks were slid into the icehouse by means of boards and pulleys and stacked layer upon layer from floor to ceiling. Sawdust was spread between each layer for insulation and to keep the blocks from sticking together. In the deep of winter, men were already busy preparing for the next summer season with the ice harvest. (Courtesy of the Silver Bay Association.)

EPILOGUE

Our pictorial journey ends in the late 1920s. Significant events were beginning to alter the lifestyle portrayed on these pages and were to continue doing so for the next two decades. The prosperity that followed World War I permitted the emergence of the automobile as a primary means of transportation for a broad cross section of the population. New roads were built to facilitate travel, including the completion of a route over Tongue Mountain in 1928, which finally connected towns along the entire western shoreline.

With added mobility, vacationing habits changed. The long-term vacation spent in one place gave way to short stays in a variety of locations. Lake George was no longer the playground of just the affluent. Less expensive tourist accommodations were also desired, and small roadside cabins appeared. Decreased revenues at the old hotels and aging boardinghouses did not permit them to be maintained, and over a period of years most fell victim to fire or were torn down.

The stock market crash of 1929 and the Great Depression also caused financial hardship. Large steamer trunks no longer were piled high on the lake's steamer docks, and mail and freight contracts were carried year-round over the newly constructed roads. Due to the drastic decline in steamboat revenues, the Delaware & Hudson scrapped the *Sagamore* in 1937 and the *Horicon* in 1939. Only the smaller *Mohican* remained. The railroad train that had replaced the stagecoach in 1882 gradually met its own demise, as passengers dwindled in number. Train service was reduced in the 1940s and entirely discontinued in 1957. The railroad right-of-way was subsequently sold.

World War II marked the end of the era pictured here and the beginning of another. Following the war, many of the former hotels, boardinghouses, and fashionable estates were replaced by new modern motels, cottage colonies, and a proliferation of small restaurants and shops. Since then, shifts in lifestyle and accommodation preferences have continued to evolve; yet, with all the changes that have taken place over the years, the lake has managed to retain its allure. Its picturesque natural beauty so vividly described in travel journals centuries ago continues to enchant. Guard it well!